Altars and Icons

Altars and Icons

SACRED SPACES IN EVERYDAY LIFE

BY JEAN McMANN

CHRONICLE BOOKS

SAN FRANCISCO

Library of Congress Cataloging-in-Publication Data
McMann, Jean.
Altars and icons: sacred spaces in everyday life / by Jean McMann;
photography by Jean McMann.
124 p.   19 x19 cm.
ISBN 0-8118-1816-0 (hardcover)
1. Shrines. 2. Spiritual biography. I. Title.
BL580.M46   1998
291.3'7 — dc21   97-34409
                                                                 CIP

Printed in Hong Kong.

Designed by Rowan Moore, Cover Collage by J.W. Morris, DoubleM Ranch

Distributed in Canada by Raincoast Books
8680 Cambie Street
Vancouver, British Columbia V6P 6M9

10 9 8 7 6 5 4 3 2 1

Chronicle Books
85 Second Street
San Francisco, California 94105

Web Site: www.chronbooks.com

CONTENTS

For Nina Payne, dear friend and fellow artist
with thanks and love

Introduction

The first altars I remember making were in the empty stable at the back fence of our half acre when I was eight or nine. We lived in Chico, California, a hot Central Valley town filled with trees. I loved to dream in the stable and play in its two broken stalls, which still smelled of horse and hay and dried-out manure. Into each stall I put a wooden crate, right at the center. I searched through the tangle of old shirts and dresses in the rag bag at the back of my mother's closet, picked out red rayon and yellow flowered cotton, ripped off sleeves and belts and collars to make smooth squares. From a shelf in the dark cellar, with its slightly rotten scent of old jam, I took two small, empty jars. Squatting outside in the glare, I filled them with hot water from the hose and added a few orange nasturtiums, with their green leaves and endearing tendrils, and some pink baby roses.

I carried my tablecloths and bouquets out to the stable and placed them carefully on the boxes, one in each of the stalls. When they were perfectly arranged, I sat down on the last, broken-down hay bale, taking them in, dreaming. I played (or *worked) this way many times, always alone. I think now that these little tables were offerings to a god of beauty, order, and home. Each cloth just so, the flowers, three or four, in the jar, on the cloth, in the center of the crate, exactly in the center of each little room. This place was mine. Inside, I was safe from my younger sisters and exhausted mother, dwelling in what poet Donald Hall calls "the momentary grace of order."*

Today, in my California garden, five Tibetan bells hang from the branches of an old pear tree. Face to face on the ledge at the foot of my computer screen, two tiny Zuni bears carry treasures on their backs. On the corner of a chest in the living room there are pictures of my grandmothers, a candle, and a clock that no longer tells time. In the house, the garden, even my car, I arrange and rearrange things that have private, symbolic meanings.

Has everybody done something like this at one time or another? How many people, young or old, make shrines—arrangements of those crucial tokens, talismans, and mementos we might call sacred souvenirs? These questions came up a few years ago, when I was visiting the homes of some recent immigrants to California. I noticed that the newcomers often made special displays of artifacts they'd brought with them. These small sites of memory—a Chinese scroll, a corn-grinding stone from Mexico, a bit of Irish turf—seemed to comfort and inspire them. While a few readily called their arrangements "shrines," many were at a loss for words to describe what they had done. I began to think further about my own similar arrangements at home and about the word "shrine" itself. I found dictionary definitions ranging from the general "box, coffer, cabinet, or chest" to "a specific place where a saint's relics are preserved."

Certainly the domestic arrangements I'd seen were much more than boxes or containers. Many included pictures or representations that could be called icons; some of these images were religious, others were not. Searching in my community, I found secular shrines, both reverent and irreverent, including some that were funny or even outrageous. Even those that appeared light-hearted had serious meanings for their makers. The objects were frequently connected to a person who was loved, or valued, or even feared. A thing stood in for someone who was missing, or for a longed-for place, for comfort and guidance when these were out of reach. Arranging icons, treasures, and knickknacks seemed to be a kind of sacred play, like a child's serious work with tiny toys at a sand table. Finally, I defined a shrine for myself: an ordered arrangement of objects with symbolic meaning.

Without mentioning my definition, I began to ask friends and acquaintances whether they had shrines in their houses. Many said yes right away. A few said absolutely not. Several described a collection of special things they kept on display, then asked, "But is that a shrine?" When I questioned Bronni Galin, she shook her head no. Later, she tentatively mentioned that she keeps her mother's picture on the bedroom windowsill, along with a little basket that holds seashells and the miniature Volvo license plate that reminds her of her first car (see page 34). Victoria Scott told me that she arranges objects with "subliminal content" all over her house (see page 120).

An apparently ordinary object or arrangement becomes a shrine when it is given some extra significance. In San Francisco a few years ago, a discarded concrete traffic barrier, four feet tall and weighing two tons, was considered by a few people to be a manifestation of the Hindu god Shiva. Word spread, and pilgrims from as far away as India began to visit it regularly in Golden Gate Park. When the crowds became a problem, park officials took steps to have the shrine removed. Until recently, it was installed in a neighborhood ashram that was once a garage. Now its whereabouts are a mystery.

A material thing—a stone, a photograph, an old shoe—can become a shrine when it is displayed in a way that evokes inspiration, memory, respect, or reverence. We value objects that are part of a collection for their beauty, rarity, or historical significance; the things in our shrines are valuable for the memories and sentiments they evoke. Commonplace or exotic, they return our thoughts, over and over, to something we choose to recall. A funny, heartfelt display like Ken Botto's gathering of sacred and secular goddesses is a shrine, even though it's not at all like an altar in a church or temple (see page 110). We assemble worshipful displays of both religious and popular heroes, from Mother Teresa to Elvis Presley (see page 108).

Shrines have varied life cycles, just as heroes and other living things do. They may change frequently or remain the same for years, disappear forever or be renewed periodically. People put up temporary shrines: a Christmas tree, a wedding altar, a display of keepsakes at a memorial service. By building niches into walls, erecting gravestones, and designing family chapels, we create more permanent installations. From generation to generation, we pass our relics and rituals down.

Even when customs are carefully handed down, each new generation makes marked or subtle changes. Traditional altars for the Mexican Day of the Dead, for example, vary widely from household to household and from year to year. Yet certain elements and rules persist, such as positioning a holy image (often the Virgin of Guadalupe) centrally, and placing a relative's photograph and his or her favorite foods and objects on the altar. Flowers are essential, particularly bright orange marigolds similar to the cempuasuchil blossoms used for these altars in Mexico.

Flowers have been connected with rituals for thousands of years. Petals of bright flowers seemed to form a mandala around the body in a twelve-thousand-year-old Neanderthal grave at Shanidar, in northern Iraq. Stones, too, have been sacred for thousands of years. At Lepenski Vir, in what is now Bosnia, archaeologists found a "sacral area" at the center of the small, fan-shaped houses they excavated. Sometime around 8000 B.C.E., a large, egg-shaped boulder was placed upright at that spot. Excavating small Neolithic houses at nearby Opovo, built several thousand years later, archaeologist Ruth Tringham inferred that the ovens she found in each served as shrines. She saw these shrines as vital to the continuation of the social order in that prehistoric community. A simple oven "takes on great significance as the source of all the energy of birth, death, fortune, and misfortune for the woman who sits next to it," she writes.

Ancient humans, it seems, set great store by their objects and the ordinary acts that put them to use. The things they made and gathered were precious—many, if not most, were used for sacred purposes. So much of life was sacred: eating, hunting, perhaps all the daily activities were consecrated to the gods. In traditional cultures, at least until recent times, some of these ancient beliefs have maintained their power. Celebrating our seasonal holidays, blowing out birthday candles, and knocking on wood, we perpetuate them.

Forms and practices from other cultures, past and present, have always inspired shrine makers. There are people who object to this borrowing, pointing out that customs and rituals from other cultures and other eras are usually mistranslated and at best only partially understood. They are correct. Still, ideas cannot be contained within boundaries; humans and their customs inevitably mingle and transform each other. A shrine is not only a portrait or mirror of its maker, it is also a reflection of the complicated, global culture that surrounds us.

To make a shrine, no matter how simple, is to make art—not for profit, but as a gift. Like singing, praying, swearing, and whistling, to assemble and arrange things we care for is a human urge. Poised alone at the millennium, many individuals are turning for comfort and stability to the ancient powers of objects: not the glossy consumer items we are encouraged to buy, but the priceless, tarnished relics of personal and family histories. These things represent our triumphs, our epiphanies, our tragic losses; we cherish them, display them, and endow them with magic.

A photograph rarely reveals these magical powers, but the camera can capture beauty, inventiveness, reverence, and whimsy. In this book, I have tried to photograph each shrine simply and clearly, without changing its form or creating an artificial atmosphere. Whenever possible, I've used available light, often a mixture of daylight and incandescent lamps, and photographed the shrine in its usual location, including reflections, cobwebs, and other phenomena of ordinary life.

For me, each of the shrines in this book has a personality, revealed through its particular shapes, colors, and textures. Even a stranger can read meaning in a portrait, the gesture of a signature, a handwritten note. Placement is also revealing: some of the objects seem to have alighted spontaneously; others have the stance of a thing that has made a planned landing. Some are new, many are smoothed and smudged by time and the touch of hands, as though they have been picked up and replaced many times. However different we are from each other, our objects cheer and inspire us, sadden us, keep us company, remind us of what we care about. Arranging and celebrating them, we give shape to our world, visible and invisible.

CHAPTER *1*

This arrangement on the old chest in our living room honors some close relatives who have died. I made it just before Halloween, the time of year when many ancient cultures communicated with ghosts and departed spirits. Because my heritage is Scottish-Irish and I grew up in California, where no one tradition dominates, mine is a nontraditional, Anglo shrine. Still, I was strongly inspired by the way many Mexican families honor relatives who have died. Their custom of making altars for the Days of the Dead, with flowers, gifts, and a deceased relative's favorite food and drink, has spread north across the border into our western and southwestern states.

Doug, my husband, was about thirteen when he took the black-and-white photograph of his father holding a fish. His brother, Gary, is in the color snap-shot, smiling. Gary died six years ago at forty-six, two years after their father. My mother and father are on the top tier, hand-colored in their wedding clothes.

My father craved Mounds bars; my mother loved Constant Comment tea. For Gary, there's a pack of Camels; Budweiser was Doug's father's favorite drink.

These objects transform the top of our chest into a site of memory. I think of private landscapes like this one as querencias, *places that hold the heart. The word has been translated as homing instinct and affection. Expatriate Alastair Reid introduced me to it in 1965, writing about the Spanish bullfight in the* New Yorker. *After the first wound, the bull chooses his querencia, that place in the ring where he returns for a moment to rest before the fight goes on, and where he finally dies.* Querencia *comes from the common Spanish verb* querer; *among its many meanings are to love, to want, to hold, and to command. Reid spoke of hometowns and native countries as* querencias; *exiles cling to their memories of them. Because these places and the people who lived there are never the same as they were, our longing for them can never be fulfilled. Photographs of places and people in our pasts often bring up that familiar sense of loss.*

When I glance in passing at my father and mother in the picture frame, thoughts play across my mind. Some circle back again and again: I wonder what happened to her hand-colored wedding dress; I think of the blonde, prickly hairs on the backs of his fingers. Mixing past with present, this landscape on the top of the chest holds pieces of my history. I can, if I wish, set images at certain angles, Grandma facing Grandpa, my young father leaning against my old father. I can change them now and then, giving old memories new contexts. In this way I remember what I want to remember, forget what I need to forget.

Eleanor Coppola

Each object, each piece of fabric on this altar makes me think of something I especially value. That lower photograph represents my treasured relationship with Gia, my son Gio's child. The picture above it shows me with Gio on Mother's Day, May 12, 1986, the last day we spent together before he was killed in the boating accident. He brought me nine bouquets of flowers that day, as if he was making up for all of the teenage stuff he pulled on me. He got a haircut a few days later, but I like to imagine him this way, a little scruffy, as though he's transforming into an angel, with angelic curly hair. The intense red roses remind me of him, too; Gio always chose red roses. There are a lot of red tones on this altar. I'm not sure why I've saved those dead flowers for so long. I suppose it's because I like their funny purple deadness as a counterpoint to the living flowers.

The picture at the very top is from a happy occasion, the family with five members before we became a family of four. I put it in the highest position because my adult life has been dominated by this family and its configuration with and without Gio. The fringed red textile is from the Philippines, where we all went to shoot *Apocalypse Now*. That was my first experience in a non-Western culture. What a pivotal time in my life! I also have gifts here from all three of my children. Because Francis's personality is so visible, larger than life, the kids know exactly who he is. When they give me a present that shows they see me, it means a lot, because I never feel totally secure about being able to communicate who I am.

The little chubby white face is a sandstone sculpture of me as a child. It was made by my father, who was an artist. He was always making things—it reminds me of my love of doing things with my hands. I sometimes get so busy that all I do with my hands is write faxes. So I try to remember that part of my history.

Behind the sculpture there's a black battery from a state-of-the-art digital video camera Francis gave me recently. He's always on the cutting edge of technology, and I treasure the way his gifts bring me along. There's also a sweet valentine from him hidden inside that wooden box at the center, along with other memorabilia. In fact, some of the most important elements in this shrine are not visible, including an article my mother wrote about wisdom. Inside that crocheted container on top of the box is a stone wrapped in wishes we made on New Year's Day. My aspirations for the year are cooking in that little container.

I love having this altar because of the sentiments I associate with it. But there's also something very soothing in just placing objects, shifting their position, or refolding the fabric, making the square a little smaller or a little larger. It satisfies some artistic part of myself. I used to feel embarrassed about making altars—I wish there were a word that spoke of their deep meaning without sounding so religious. I think of an altar as a place where you commune with God or whatever you believe in. I suppose I consider that God is in everything, even that red fringe.

Eleanor Decker

FIREPLACE ALTARS FOR THE DAYS OF THE DEAD

In making my shrines for the Days of the Dead this year I've honored our cow, Dottie. Naturally there's a portrait of Dottie that shows what she really looked like, and then there are angel Dotties. Her spirit can come and take the carrot spirit from the carrots and the apple spirit from the apples. The little asters were her favorite flowers; she always stole them from the garden. The cowbell is a birthday gift my friend Ruth brought to the big cow birthday party we had when Dottie turned twenty.

On the mantel up above Dottie's shrine, is a wonderful, ghostly picture of my mother and father together in London. I have always loved that picture because they looked ghostly even then—so perfect for the Days of the Dead. My father is holding his coat closed against what must have been a cold windy day—it's a sweet gesture and it does not remind me of my father at all.

I have animal images to honor my dead dogs and cats, the many Mexican things in honor of Mexico and what we learned when we lived there. And I always include figures of musicians because it's a good thing for all these creatures and people to have a little music.

Mary Priest

LAVENDER WALK

Everything here was just put. No intention of making a shrine whatsoever; just a gathering of things I love that give me some sort of stability. It's like walking past a lavender bush every day; you feel the dry blossoms, and you smell your hand. These are icons in their way, I suppose. You pick them up and give them a whole new dimension by saying, "Hey, you're here."

The first thing I put on the table was the photo of John and me just married, standing rather pensively on the steps of the Cathedral in Washington, D.C., in 1960. I didn't get the photograph of Daddy—it's right at the center—until Mummy had died, because she loved it and didn't want to give it away. The picture was taken just before he was shipped off to the trenches in World War I. He is eighteen years old, in the uniform of the Scottish Black Watch. If you look closely, you can see the questioning terror as well as the shyness and diffidence in his eyes. Today is the first time I have looked, really looked into those eyes.

It's very difficult being the first one over when you emigrate. I always felt guilty, felt I deserted England and my family. I had no one here. So this table says, Even though I'm new here I have a very long, deep past in another country. I brought it over and I will try and carry it on. In a funny way, this table is my little English village church. I haven't got the tombstones; I have this instead.

Franco Mondini Ruiz

WATER FOR THE SPIRITS OF DANNY AND DREW

What I've created is something between an altar and an *ofrenda*. It's an altar in the sense that it's a shrine to the memory of Drew Allen and Danny Lozano, two of my very close friends and mentors who died in the last few years. It has two *cazuelas* (two dishes of water), placed in front of a silver paper collage by my friend Alejandro Diaz. I learned about the water from my mother — in the Mexican tradition you leave out dishes of water for the spirits of the dead. They're thirsty, and they sometimes come back craving the goodies they loved during their lives. So you calm and appease them with an *ofrenda*, an offering.

I grew up in a modern suburban household here in San Antonio, but the old Mexican ways of dealing with spirituality often carried through. To us, it was very possible that our favorite cat had the spirit of our grandmother after she died. We were raised with this comforting way of thinking, that there were souls and spirits all around you, spirituality and animism mixed with typical Catholic dogma. At the same time, my mother, my grandmother, even my great-grand-mother, wanted to become more modern, more Americanized in some ways. To them, a new refrigerator was more important and more beautiful than an *ofrenda* or a shrine—maybe our Sears refrigerator was my grandmother's altar.

My own altar represents a very fast cultural journey. It wasn't until relatively recently, when I was in my twenties, that I started learning about "high" Mexican culture—pre-Columbian art, Frida Kahlo, Diego Rivera, altars, *ofrendas*, folk art, all of that. I learned about the richness of my heritage mostly from Anglos like Drew Allen, the cultural aesthetes of our city. It was pretty much a rich Anglo thing. The most painful part of growing up in San Antonio was that so many of the cultural elite loved the *form* of Mexican culture, but didn't give Mexican Americans any credit for having the substance. When young Latinos like myself were eventually exposed to it, we were totally seduced, not only by the beauty of our heritage, but by its substance, its mean-ing, as well. And we were just crushed by the realization that we'd been taught to be ashamed of what could have made us so proud. In this region a lot of us went from that ignorance to becoming collectors of Mexican art along with the Anglos. And eventually we began to see our heritage as not only Mexican, or Mexican American, but part of something much larger—a world culture. Now we're making altars that are mixtures of all the things we grew up with, includ-ing pop art, minimalism, Zen Buddhism, Native American ideas, even the Brady Bunch.

Recently I was thinking about how my shrine, to look its best, requires water almost to the very brim. I always maintain the shrine when I pass by, by filling up the two bowls on the altar. And as I do that I get a bowl for myself—the cold tap water is so delicious. It's almost like having communion with your friends. You're having a drink with them, even if it's just water. And I think about Danny and Drew, as they're getting their water and I'm getting mine. It's as though they're looking out for me. You see, about three years ago I really let myself get dehydrated, and I almost died. I still don't drink enough water, and now that daily ritual of passing by the altar is just one more reminder to give myself the water I need.

Amalia and Carlos Vasquez

ALTAR ON THE STAIRWAY,
DEDICATED TO THE DEAD ONES
IN OUR FAMILY

Amalia: I made this altar with my son Carlos, who's twelve; it's a tradition for people from Oaxaca, Mexico, to make an altar for the *Días de Los Muertos,* the Days of the Dead. We usually put ours up about October 31, and we keep it up, with the candle burning, until November 5. For us it's a happy time—on November 1 or 2 all the Vasquez family in the area have dinner together. Everybody eats mole, chocolate, and tortillas.

We put the altar in the corner at the top of the stairs; it's the only place we have room for it in our apartment. I make the chicken mole. In Mexico they kill the chicken, and they grind the chocolate by hand. Everything is fresh, nothing is commercial, the way it is here. But I add extra things to the package.

Carlos: Sometimes I make the chocolate, and I go to the *panadería* to buy the bread. I couldn't make the mole or the tamales. I like making the altar because it's fun and it always looks nice after we're done.

Amalia: We always put flowers on it. In Mexico we used the yellow and orange *cempuasuchil*. And there's a flower called *flor de muerto* that grows wild in the countryside. It has a very strong odor; all the houses in Mexico smell of it during Days of the Dead. We used other flowers, big red ones called *cresta de gallo*; I've never seen them here in the United States. When you're in another place you have to change, so here we buy roses, red roses, and marigolds.

The altar is for all the people in the family who have died, not just one person. This year we have dedicated the altar especially to my husband's mother, Valeria Garnica Molina. She died two years ago, on the twenty-sixth of November.

Carlos: I don't remember how my grandma looked, so the picture reminds me. That's the most important thing—the altar reminds me of the people in my family who are dead.

Amalia: On the altar we have the Virgin of Juquila, a small town in the state of Oaxaca, and Carmen, the Virgin of the Sailors; we bought her in Oaxaca City. We have water for the spirits to drink. And there is mezcal and tequila and beer, some delicious things they liked when they were alive. We have cigarettes and matches, so the men can smoke. We have nuts, and the special *pan*, the bread for the Days of the Dead, and chocolate, and fruits—banana, guava, peach. The fruit smells wonderful on the altar. We should have sugar cane, but it is very expensive here. We have to be economical. In Mexico we made a much bigger altar, a whole table.

My husband, Jesus, and I want Carlos to learn how to make the altar, so he can carry on the tradition when he's married. Next year he will be able to do this by himself.

Carlos: When I'm twenty or twenty-one, I'll probably have my own altar.

Amalia: But only I can make the mole!

Andrew Romanoff

I put these things out in 1991, when Russia opened up. Until then, they were all in drawers. It was a self-conscious sort of thing, I'd say, about not wanting to face my heritage. Before then it was too painful. But now, since I've been to Russia, I feel much freer—there's a sense of relief. I put some Russian earth in those little plastic film containers because I wanted to have it around me, close by. I have soil from Ekaterinburg, the place where the czar was murdered. I also have a canister of soil from each of the five palaces where the royal family lived, and stones I gathered at those sites. You see, Nicholas II, the Czar of Russia, was my granduncle; my grandmother, Grand Duchess Xenia, was his sister.

The photographs here are of my mother and father, my father in uniform, and my grandmother on horseback. The photograph of my granddaughter Natasha, on the right-hand side, is a recent addition. The black-and-white cross is a memento of my arrival in Ekaterinburg in 1992. I was the first one of the Romanoffs to visit the site—I was invited to go with the film crew for the movie *The Mystery of the Last Czar*. When seven of us arrived in Ekaterinburg at three in the morning, a group with the vice mayor met us and gave us flowers. They told us, "Since our town has been closed all these years, we don't really know how to treat visitors from outside." The cross is made of Ural stones—it was given to me by the son-in-law of Alexander Avdonin, who worked with Geli Ryabov on the excavation of the remains of the czar's bones in 1976. Avdonin and his brother are geologists, and his brother gave me about a dozen stones from the Ural mountains. I have them displayed here.

Once in a while I find a beautiful crystal, or somebody gives me one, and I put it on display, too. And I have Winkie the koala bear lying up there on the top shelf—a stuffed toy that was given to me when I was six years old by Princess Victoria, the granddaughter of Queen Victoria. Most of the other objects in that cabinet were given to me by my wife, Inez Storer, who is an artist, my children, and other family members. I hope that one of the kids will keep all of these things and cherish them.

John Kriken

THE TRAVEL WHATNOT

I don't know if these objects are tiny metaphors, but this whatnot represents a kind of coming together of experiences mostly connected with my work as a city planner. I also call it a crèche, which comes from living in Texas and seeing a lot of real crèches in people's gardens and houses. Once in Mexico I was flying in an airplane and inside the pilot's cockpit I saw two beautiful little ceramic pieces glued to one of the side panels. One piece even had a candle coming out of it. The juxtaposition of the airplane control panel and the crèche was wonderful—religion and technology. I felt very safe.

This is a kind of display cabinet for the Chinese home that I bought in Hong Kong in the 1970s. I was looking for a place to keep things that remind me of events I've experienced and places I've been. In the whatnot, I try to synthesize all the different places and cultures I'm working with. Things I've collected are put here together for hundreds of different reasons I can't even explain. They're all very inexpensive. A lot have to do with memories—the little ship is a memory of the time when I used to be a sailor on a merchant ship that looked just like that. And on the shelf below the cabinet is something very, very special: my father's sextant. It guided him around the world—he was a sea captain, and he used it to take sightings of the stars.

All of these pieces signify places existing simultaneously in the world, and every piece is a mystery to me. In that sense the cabinet is a sort of religious object, in that it's mysterious and kind of beyond my grasp. That's really what I like about it; that there's no consistent set of ideas here. With all the pretty stuff we have in the house to look at, it's funny that I spend so much time looking at this. Out of all the tiny bits I usually focus on one or two objects. Each time I come back from a trip I might put one more thing up on this shelf. Maybe it's a way of looking at all the cultures and the pieces of the world. With this one little visual array I can think, "Oh my God, how does it all fit together?"

Maya Vasquez

MEMORABILIA

This is basically a collection of memorabilia, things that are meaningful to me but not specifically related to my faith or the connection I feel with God. My mother-in-law, Valeria Garnica Molina, gave me the picture of the Virgin; she had a great deal of faith in the Virgin of Juquila. I'm interested in traditional pictures of virgins, but I don't believe in the whole concept of the virginity of Mary. The image is a way of remembering my mother-in-law. And here are a few little saints from my sister-in-law, Amelia, who lives in Oaxaca. They're simpler images, very meaningful to her.

Most of the other things are knickknacks: little things we brought back from Oaxaca, a plaque a friend gave me when the boys were baptized, a Mary and baby Jesus music box given to Lydia when she was baptized. These have more to do with memory than faith.

I'm not a traditionally Catholic person. I'd rather find the holy in the human beings we see every day, instead of gold-leafed images. But it's good for my kids to know what those statues are. It's as much a connection with their past as with their future—they're half Mexican, they live in the United States, and I'm North American. It's important to pass your worldview and your culture on to your kids. My mother passed her culture on to me, for instance, and I've taken it and done something else with it. That probably happens with each generation, as long as people are thinking and reflective.

Bronni Galin

The small photograph of my mother is my favorite picture of her. She looks to me like an old lady, but when it was taken she was younger than I am now. I was about fifteen then. She didn't live too much longer after that; she died when she was sixty-one. I really love the picture of my mother and me together. I love her pride in me. She was forty-one when I was born. Think of it; she thought she could never have a baby because she had been married before she married my father and had never been pregnant, ever. I was the only child she had, so I grew up with that feeling of being somebody's treasure. I was very serious, though. In all the photos of me that's the most smile you'll ever see.

I meditate here in the morning, between the bed and this windowsill. Afterward, I bow to the dust ruffle on the bed and then I bow to the empty wall, which is where I imagine my father. And then I turn around to bow to my mother's picture, and I feel a difference in my face and in my being when I do that. I never think of myself as religious, and "shrine" feels like a very religious word. So I wouldn't have thought in those terms; I never thought of this windowsill as a shrine until you said the words. But it is. I think it is.

Terry A. Ybañez

ALTAR DE MIS MEMORIAS DE MIS QUERIDOS
(Altar of My Memories of My Loved Ones)

About fifteen years ago, when I was twenty-two, I started this altar in memory of my grandfather Pomposa Reyna. He was long dead—if he'd been alive he would have been in his hundred-somethings. Five years later, I added Elena Reyes, my mother's mother, to the altar. I had just gotten a palm reading from my Uncle Alfredo, who's a *curandero*, a healer. He said my dead grandmother Elena was my guardian angel; I should start including her in my altar or no more guardian angel!

In the past three years many of my friends have passed away, some from AIDS, others from cancer or old age. It was overwhelming to suddenly lose so many friends, so I started including them in the altar as well. Now I keep my altar for deceased friends and family in the front room all the time. My mother finds it very strange to find all these dead people here. She thinks my altars are very pretty, but a little morbid. She likes it that I include my grandparents, but she always asks, "Why do you have all these other people?" The fact is, sometimes I feel closer to my friends than I do to my blood family. My mother's and grandmother's altars all focused on their children. But I don't have children, so mine focuses on people who had a very positive influence on my life and on other people's lives.

My mother is a very devout Catholic. She has always had an altar with the Virgin Mary and Jesus on it. It wasn't until later that she added the Virgin of Guadalupe. Now her altar includes Guadalupe and photographs of her family, her kids, and her grandchildren.

My father's mother, my grandmother Maria, had an altar with a white Virgin Mary, very beautiful, but there was no Virgin of Guadalupe. She had a Jesus figure, San Antonio, Saint Francis of the Birds, and San Martin with all the animals gathered around him. She had candles, too, and if she was making a request on someone's behalf, she'd have that person's picture.

She also had a big cement Buddha sitting in her garden, surrounded by herb plants. When I was five years old, it was nearly my height. I was always fascinated with this Buddha because he was in a yoga position with his eyes closed, and his fingers looked like lotus flowers. Buddha has been in my life since I was a baby, and now I have my own Buddhist shrine in my hallway. My grandmother collected Buddhas and elephants as aesthetic objects; they didn't have any spiritual meaning. She liked Buddha for the same reason I do, because he looks so happy.

The three of us, myself, my mother, and my grandmother Maria Reyna who passed away recently, have had different altars and very different ways of remembering our deceased. I guess that shows you the generational cycle, but it also shows how a younger generation returns to what they know, or sometimes to what they didn't know. It's interesting how things come around in a circle.

CHAPTER  2 CELEBRATING HEARTH AND HOME

A shrine can grow out of the structure of a house: a doorway, a shelf above the kitchen sink, a cup rail high on the wall around the dining room. Mantels, built over the vestigial fire at the core of a dwelling, are now picture frames for things we want to display. Sometimes a mantel is one family member's territory, not to be violated by unauthorized objects. Or the arrangement may be a joint effort, representing a whole family. Home displays such as Christmas trees, menorahs, and Kwanzaa tables may reinforce family and community values.

At my house we don't have a fireplace with a mantel, only the top of the black, pot-bellied stove, where a teapot rests in winter or holds flowers in the path of summer light. I don't remember Doug ever placing something on the stove. He says he thinks of it as mine, and I let him. What I see as our fireplace shrine is a black ceramic bowl on the floor. I am gradually filling it with round sea stones, one carried home for each walk we take to the ocean.

5. White rose from the garden.

2. Persimmon:
My mother often had a bowl of them
on the dining room table.

6. Stone:
Jean's card came with a present, but to me
the small clear picture of the lichen-covered
rock was the present.

1. Mirror:
Tin-framed,
from India.
Silver upon silver.
I love mirrors.

3. Hyacinth bulbs in blue glass containers:
Christmas gifts for my neighbors. Light comes through the glass and I watch the roots grow.

4. Waxed linen basket from Nina:
Earth basket with African beads. Dust clings to the wax.
Nina wants me to wash it, but I like to see the dust on it.

7. Chinese dolls picture:
I like the warm colors
in this photograph;
the dolls sit close
together like friends.

8. *Cat cardboard:*
   Cut out of a catfood box four years ago.
   Watches all. I notice his eyes often.

10. *Birds:*
   Three, plastic, one needs a battery, one still sings
   when jostled or sometimes suddenly when the wind blows.

9. *Small totem horse from Jean:*
   Sent to take care of me while I took care of my mother.
   It cares for me.

12. *Black jug, a gift from Oaxaca:*
   Round, can't stand.
   Soft and burnished by hand.
   When I hold it I see water flow
   from it onto the windowsill.

Elaine James

KITCHEN WINDOWSILL

11. *Elephant from India:*
   I love India, the color, the dust.

Judy Booth and Jim Kraft

FRIENDS AND WITNESSES

Judy: I'm the dishwasher, so I see the three Polaroid pictures above the sink quite constantly. The whole area is related to friends, not just the Polaroids.

Jim: The one on the right is my mother in front of a tar paper tepee out near Flagstaff, Arizona.

Judy: She was an incredible friend.

Jim: Opposite her is my good friend William holding up a dead duck. William has always been a hero of mine; I've known him forever. He's one of the most frugal people in the world. He's a *rasquache* artist, like we are. For me he's a model of how to fashion things out of the most humble materials in the most economical way.

Judy: Rasquachismo has to do with taking something you have and using it in a different manner, like the old bowling balls we're using to build a wall out-side.

Jim: It also has to do with making things from scratch; the word comes from the Spanish verb *rascar,* to scratch or scrape.

Judy: Almost all the little bits and pieces here have very personal meanings for me.

Jim: The little picture in the middle is a photo of me and our good friend Holly posing as used car salesmen. That has to do with remembering a curious point in time when we were all younger and funnier. Those Indian things around the window are a reflection of influences that have come to us from various places. Each little beaded figure represents a source of strength or informa-tion. What we're really talking about is a reverence for the past, for people and things that remind us of that, even in an indirect way.

Judy: The integration of the daily world and the shrine world, the sacred world, is an incredibly important part of it all. That's what gives you something back.

Adam Troy Ahumada

PAGAN ALTAR

I'm Puerto Rican, so I've grown up with alternative spiritual beliefs. My parents came to New York from an island where there are very strong magical practices. Some of my family were Presbyterian, others were Catholic, and some were really into voodoo and the blacker arts. Objects given to me by family members and close friends have always been a part of my altar, and they are very precious to me. For instance, I have a ring from my grandfather, who passed away last year. The Snoopy toy on the mantel belongs to Zann, my roommate; he dug it up in his garden as a child.

I think of this as a pagan altar. It represents what's going on right now, but I also have things that traverse my whole life span, like the candles on the first shelf with the *Niño de Atocha* symbol. That's a very Latin image, the boy Jesus. It represents my male aspect, and the fact that I am very childlike inside, even at thirty-four. On the second shelf is my tarot card, the Knight of Wands. Even though the flames may be engulfing him, the Knight of Wands maintains dignity and self-assurance and courage. My young life was really horrible, and I'm still going through the flames. There's death on this altar, too. A very, very close and good friend gave the AIDS candle to me. AIDS is a big part of my own life right now.

The ritual I do when I sit at my altar takes ten to thirty minutes, to make myself very calm, say my little prayer that I learned from twelve-step programs, and to show my gratitude for being alive and breathing. All these things are tools for living. When I'm asking "Why, why, why?" the altar reminds me that sometimes you have to find peace within yourself without the answers. I think the whole purpose of having altars is to remember that we are here on this earth, but there are many things we don't see.

Mildred Howard

KWANZAA TABLES

I grew up celebrating Christmas; my family is from the South. We were a really large family and my mother decorated our house very ornately—the inside and the outside. We had tons of lights and Santa Claus music blasting out into the neighborhood. People would come from all over to see the house. It was exciting, but as an adult and a parent I wanted another way to celebrate, a way that spoke more about African Americans.

I first learned about Kwanzaa in the late sixties. It was a time when identity was a real issue—we had the Free Speech Movement, and a lot of civil rights were being addressed. That's when I really began to see Christmas differently. I felt its purpose was being lost in commercialism, and I didn't want to participate in that kind of activity. I started to look at other traditions that related more to my way of thinking.

I made my first Kwanzaa shrine in the early seventies. I was a single parent, I was raising two kids, and I couldn't afford anything else. The holiday was created in the midsixties by Ron Karenga; he built it on rituals from African harvest festivals. It starts on the twenty-sixth of December and lasts for seven days. Each day we light a candle and focus on a different principle: Umoja (unity), Kujichagulia (self-determination), Ujima (collective work), Ujamma (cooperative economics), Nia (purpose), Kuumba (creativity), and Imani (faith).

The Kwanzaa shrine on my kitchen table is about food. It is also about place, about who we are and how we fit in the world. There are seven candles, one for each of the principles. The red signifies the blood of African Americans and the roots that run through us, the green is for the land, and the black is for the people. I have fruits and vegetables for the harvest, and some other things that relate particularly to black Americans, like cane syrup from Georgia and watermelon and yam, which were introduced to this country by slaves. I also have a photograph of my son, Amir, the twin brother of my daughter, Timiza. He was killed in an automobile accident in 1993. It's important to give praise to those who went before you and also those who passed away. There's an Aunt Jemima image, part of my collection of black stereotypes. At one time I thought I could collect all of them because I felt so bad about them. But no way could I do that!

My second shrine, in the sitting room, has the traditional straw mat, all the fruits and vegetables, the seven candles, and some gifts. I made the two feet for an exhibition I had underneath the Brooklyn Bridge. I placed a thousand feet there on a bed of rock. The show was a result of my feeling so overwhelmed by the number of homeless people, especially the young black males. I made all the feet white because I was thinking about *no color*—that everybody is the same color in spirit.

John Moore

THE MANTEL — LIFE'S MEMORIES

I walk every morning. I've got a route from here down to the lake, around Lake Merritt and back. As I walk I'm looking all around, everywhere. And almost every day I find at least a penny. Sometimes I find a nickel or a quarter, but I love to find a penny because that's what I'm supposed to get. I find other stuff, too, and I just pick it up and bring it home and put it someplace in the house.

If I find a shell, it goes on the mantel with the shells. If I get another spoon, it goes down with the spoons. If I get more round disks, they go with the round disks. Dice go with dice. When there's an empty space I put something in it. "Oh yeah, that's where it goes." I found the little plastic ivy in the street and brought it down here, and later I picked up the pinecone. It seemed like it should sit on top of the ivy. I had the robin's eggs before I had the nest; they were sitting here all along and after the nest fell out of the tree in the back-yard, I just dropped them in. It's strange how things end up here.

I'll tell you something that was *really* strange. A friend of mine came over to play some dominoes. I'd lost a peg on my cribbage board; I was using a match-stick. And my friend saw me using the matchstick. He said, "What are you doing with that?" and he went in his pocket — I swear to God — and he gave me

a peg that fit with the others. He said he just picked it up someplace; he had no idea why. Things seem to come here because they belong here. Sometimes it gives me kind of an eerie feeling, but then you shouldn't question it because that's how things are supposed to happen.

I don't know why I have that picture of my father up there. I guess that's where he belongs. I think I got the photograph after he had passed. That totem with the A on it I made in remembrance of my friend Mildred's son, Amir. He was killed in an automobile accident. The fish represents Jesus; it's a Christian sym-

bol. The nails are for power, and the dice is for chance. Fate. The painting is called *Leopard and Stag*. It just caught my eye and I liked it. It looks almost like a real painting rather than a reproduction. Most everybody who comes here comments on it. All this other art and stuff, they might not see, but they see that painting.

When I lived in this house with my family as a teenager, none of this was on the mantel. It was a formal house. We probably had candles and photographs; I remember this silver candlestick. Otherwise, this is all my own adult junk.

Cristine Guthrie

OUR WEDDING ALTAR

This was for an absolutely impromptu marriage ceremony that John Abelson and I arranged two days before I was to begin chemotherapy. Before I knew I had cancer, we were planning a wedding in Venice in April. On Friday we decided to get married here and now, in San Francisco in December. We had the ceremony on Sunday. The next day we both had our heads shaved—John shaved his to keep me company—and the day after that I started chemotherapy.

In the middle of the mantel, holding the oil lamp, is a dish of lovely, smooth sea stones from a trip to Greece last summer. The cat candlestick is there in honor of our three cats, especially Jeepers and Peepers, the kittens. In the background to the left, next to a picture of John and me in Venice a few years ago, is the wedding certificate. It was designed by our friends Ina and Victor, and it's a very elegant thing, signed by the ten people who were there with us. They were all asked to speak or bring something for the altar, and the angel was brought by Ina. It's one of my favorite objects. The wedding candle near the center was lit to begin the ceremony. Our friend Helen sent us the little bride and groom candle—we probably won't light it because we like it too much.

The photographs on the mantel are mostly old. My parents when they got married during the Second World War, with my father wearing his Air Force uniform. My grandfather, next to his wedding picture with my grandmother. There's John with his grandson below, and a small snapshot of John as a boy with his father, probably taken in Washington State. He was born there when his father was working as an engineer on the Grand Coulee Dam.

I don't know the history of that pocket watch, or if it's actually old; I just like how it looks. A very sweet guy from Portugal who used to work in my lab gave it to me at a wonderful party the lab had for me on my fiftieth birthday. It just seemed like the right object for the shrine, although according to him it doesn't have any history.

Meridel Rubenstein and Jerry West

MUD ROOM SHRINE,
THE EVER-EVOLVING CELEBRATORY ARRAY

Meridel: The mud room is the room between the outside and the inside. You know, where you get rid of the mud? It also was our sand room because, before the road was paved, sometimes—the windy times—a cloud of sand would come into the house. Now that we've paved the road, this is a sitting room, our holiday shrine, which has evolved piece by piece and has to do with Christmas.

In fact the whole room evolved from the shrine in that closed-up window. We have some high art here, but mostly it's things we love that we've collected in our travels. We are constantly moving things around. That wonderful box with Christmas lights was made last year by our friend K. K. Cribbs. We added the cross just because we're the way we are. Now that we've traveled and been more in touch with other world religions, the room has become more devotional.

We're not your normal shrine makers; we hadn't thought we were making shrines. When you first asked about the shrine, I thought, Don't talk to me. I've never even thought about this; it's just something I do. Then I remembered my college roommate who thought I was really weird because I was always putting things up on the wall. She thought I was showing off. And then she realized that was actually the way I looked at things. It's probably true; I have always put things up to see and think about them. I'm Jewish, but there was nothing religious in my family. In fact, there was a subtle disapproval of religion. I also instinctively feel it's not quite right to have religious images. But this room is different; these objects mark things that have happened to us.

Jerry's family wasn't religious either. One of the reasons I was so drawn to him was the real strong history of traditions in his family, and how they invented their own rituals. We both love holidays—we are two people who actually love to celebrate Christmas. In November there's a festival here in Santa Fe called Shaliko. The Zunis build special Shaliko rooms in their houses, where you can look in and see them celebrating. Jerry and I have our own tradition: Each Christmas we go to the same place, we cut our tree, we get mistletoe, and we decorate this room. It becomes a kind of festival room, our version of a Shaliko room you can look into. It's not quite so stupendous that everyone in the neighborhood would want to come see it, but we just do it.

Carolyn Campagna

GRAVE STONES AND MARZIPAN

These objects connect me to people in my family who are no longer alive, including George, my dog. I really mean it; I miss my dog tremendously. There he is—his ashes are in the box on the second shelf, behind his picture. The old postcard with the waiter in a restaurant is the center of this collection of memories. My grandparents sent it to my great-grandmother in 1913 after a wonderful dinner in Rome, and years later my father sent it on to me. Here's what he wrote: "Just to let you know you're not the first member of the family enamored of Italian food." There are other, subterranean family contexts: the sample grave stone, for instance, was in my father's study all the years I remember. The green, painted egg on the shelf below belonged to Lucie. She was my much-loved French cousin who died recently at the age of ninety-four. The black marble egg next to it was my mother's. Her collection of miniature eggs always sat on her table in a duck-shaped pewter container. That duck filled with eggs always fascinated me as a child.

CHAPTER *3* AWAY FROM HOME

An auto mechanic I know is enraged that so many people collect stones and other projectiles on their dashboards. These things are dangerous, he says. For one thing, dashboard clutter has fallen on his head at work. Since he said this, I've limited myself to a few lightweight but significant items in my car. On the shelf above the dashboard are leaves, small pebbles, and a color copy of a small Indian painting I keep in our bedroom—the bottom of a holy-looking foot. Hanging from my rearview mirror are clay beads and a Chinese fish. I'd like to think these things bring me protection and good luck, anchoring the car to something fixed, like home.

People need to feel at home no matter where they are. I've noticed messages, mascots, and companions settled on desks and in cubicles in office buildings. These semipublic arrangements seem to have private meanings. Some look spontaneous, to be taken lightly. Others, family photographs carefully combined with awards and commemorations, carry more weight. I see many of these arrangements as shrines to individual identity. They're often muted because we're not so free to speak out in the work world. Some seem intended to show who we really are, or who we want others to think we are: a good father, a thinker, a jokester, a believer, a cynic. Some offer evidence of the world outside: stones (again), vacation landscapes, pine cones, souvenirs. Quotations are pinned up: inspiring, admonishing, cynical, humorous.

In the privacy of my darkroom, I also pin up mottoes: "The perfect is the enemy of the good." "Act without doing/Work without effort." Next to my computer and writing desk, there's a pin-up board, a long narrow piece of linen-covered Cellotex. Above it hang two photographs, both showing Buddha fingers in a holy gesture; these are below an upside down sheaf of pale dried stems and seedpods Nina gave me a year ago. The sheaf and the photographs form a shrinelike column rising from the Cellotex. I've pinned up poems, photographs of Doug, my children, and a few dear friends, and at the moment Adele Oglansky's recipe for Mighty Fine Meatballs. The idea tickles me. I can't seem to throw the recipe away, even though it calls for grape jelly and gingersnaps and I will never make it. Each January I clear the board, file almost everything in my yearly memorabilia folder, and begin anew. Of course, certain crucial photographs have to be pinned up again right away.

Harrod Blank

"OH MY GOD!"

The chicken on the car door is a personal totem. I grew up with chickens, so they symbolize my past, my innocence. I got the green glass pyramid that hangs from the rearview mirror from a witch doctor in Mexico. He told me that when light shines through it onto you, you emanate good energy. That's what the car is all about. My friend Kevin named it. One day we were in Santa Cruz and all these tourists kept coming up and saying, "Oh my God! Oh my God!" Kevin said, "Harrod, that's what you should name the car." And I said, "Kevin, you're a genius."

The car is really my emotional sounding board. It's where I experience my inner peace. If a girlfriend breaks up with me, or if I'm just feeling sad, I get into the car and I make it more beautiful, or more homey. I add to its depth and make it more complete. It makes me happy to be in there creating something beautiful. If there is a religion to me, that's what it is: simply making something more beautiful. To other people it might seem trivial, like "God, that guy's got a lot of time on his hands! Wonder why he does that; he's thirty-four years old and driving a clown car!" They don't understand; it's not their reality. It's very difficult to change a machine that's inherently ugly into something organic and beautiful.

This car celebrates diversity—cultural diversity, religious diversity. I've got Buddhas and Christs, Native American things and Latino things; they all have some meaning for me. "Oh my God!" is more than just an art car in a world of normal cars; it's a reflection of the world.

Jay Yarnall

GANESHA ON THE SOUNDBOARD

One summer I had a hilarious dream. I was working at Lake Tahoe, recording the songs of my friend Bhagwan Das, the spiritual teacher. In the dream I was with Ganesha, the Hindu elephant-headed god, rampaging over the whole Tahoe Basin. Toward the end of the dream I was laughing uproariously, I was out of my body, and Ganesha was smiling at me. I woke myself up laughing.

I told Bhag the dream the next day, and he gave me this Ganesha in honor of it. I took the figure home and put him on my soundboard, which is where I work and where I meet the most obstacles. I tied that bead with the red tassel around his shoulders because it has a tiny, almost-worn-off picture of the Virgin Mary on it, and set him next to a quartz crystal. When I first come in to work in the studio I say the _Om Ghanapati Namah_ mantra, "O Great Ganesh I bow to you continuously." And I give him a polite Japanese bow.

As a child I was a secret agnostic in the Episcopalian church. My parents said I had to attend church until I was sixteen, so I went until then and quit. To me church always seemed a spooky place rather than a spiritual one. All the God stuff seemed more scary than comforting. And when I got into my teens, the irrationality of it didn't make any sense. It wasn't till the sixties hit and I took psychedelics and so on that God showed up pretty definitely.

When I broke my neck in 1967 it forced a real spiritual crisis. I was nineteen, AWOL from the navy boot camp, living with some hippie friends in the Haight Ashbury. A flower child with a crew cut. I was tripping on STP, which is a wicked psychedelic, and I jumped out a window. The whole event was part of a psychedelic drama because my STP delusions continued in the hospital for two more days. It culminated when I got out of the hellishness of it: I called on Jesus's name and broke free. And that was the first time I really felt like I believed.

I was in bed for a year. Then I was able to get up in a wheelchair, first an electric chair and finally a manual one. After five years or so I was pretty independent. During those five years I started exploring Eastern religion. One day I realized that I could spend my whole life mourning what I couldn't do, and I started to pay attention to what I could do. A vast area opened up that I probably would have ignored or just played around with if I hadn't broken my neck. Before that, spirituality was really a hobby for me rather than a focus. I was a bad drummer and a bad harmonica player—I doubt if I would have gone any farther than that. I never would have taken music or art seriously. But last Chinese New Year in the Oakland Coliseum, I saw twenty thousand people dancing to my music while the Grateful Dead played along.

Cristina Kotsovolos

JESUS, MARY, AND JOSEPH

Jesus, Mary, and Joseph were originally on the prow of a small Styrofoam boat my husband, Tim, bought at a wedding—they auctioned off these boats to raise money for the bride and groom. Recently we took the boat apart, and Tim and my brother-in-law decided to put the icon on the hood of my truck. They asked me if it was okay, and I said "Sure, I can use some protection, especially on the road." So far it has also given me good parking karma, knock on wood.

It's mostly a hood ornament, the way Cadillacs and Jaguars have hood ornaments. It also reminds me a lot of being down in Mexico, how all the buses and cars have just tons of stuff like this. We think it's kind of funny, but it's not a parody; it's not putting Jesus Christ down or anything like that. I grew up in the Greek Orthodox Church, and I've always thought of icons as things that are only in church or a shrine in your house. Having it on the truck was kind of a freeing-up of rules and regulations—freedom of expression in religion. I feel protected by this icon. That may be because it's a reminder that the road is a pretty dangerous place to be. I'm frightened of car accidents; I've been in five and I don't really want to be in any more. So I believe in it.

Beth Sawi

MY SERENITY CORNER

I'm not sure this actually started off as a shrine. I had wanted a fountain in my office ever since I saw one at the Nature Company years and years ago. It seemed to be such a wonderful, relaxing monument that I decided to reward myself with one if I ever got an office big enough. This happened about four or five years ago, after working with Charles Schwab in the discount broker-age area for over a decade. I bought this, but I couldn't decide where to place it. I had it on a variety of tables, but really more as a decorative item. When I came into this office, it found its way into this corner where the light streams in. We put some plants behind it, and the fountain suddenly turned into a shrine.

Over the years it has evolved into my serenity corner, a place in my office where I can think and relax. Once I enter the room, with the computer and telephone at hand, I go into e-mail, voice-mail, to-do mode. I need this other part of my office to pull me back out of my busy corporate existence and return me to the realm of the thoughtful.

It's not a particularly religious shrine because I'm Episcopalian. The little dragon from the Chinese New Year is here because I was born in the year of the dragon. It's one of the creative signs, and I try to bring more creativity into my work life. I feel I don't express that side of myself enough, at home or at work. A lot of what's on the table has to do with aspirations, to remind me to think creatively. The carved stones in the fountain, for instance: one on loving, one on creating, one on reaching. And these two kaleidoscopes signify that things aren't always what you see. All it takes is a little bit of a turn and your vision can totally change.

Holly Roberts

PAINTING WALL SHRINE

That wall is a sacred place to me. Over the years an incredible patina has built up; there's a trace of every painting I've made there. Making art is such a mysterious thing—you don't know what direction the rays are coming from. For me, it's the act of making art that makes a place sacred. It's not, "Oh here's a sacred place and I'm going to paint here." A space becomes sacred through creating it and shaping it and treating it with respect.

In every studio I've had, I've pinned three *milagros* on the wall above me. They are always a horse and a heart and a pair of eyes; that's the combination of who I am. My eyes see physically, but it's my heart, the passion and that emotional connection, that really sees. And the horse has always been my animal.

I think real art springs from the same channel as religion. We're drilling down to the same well, a bigger stream of power. I treat my wall and what's around it as sacred, hoping I'll be allowed into that deeper stream. I think it's deeper than the collective unconscious everyone talks about. We're all trying to tap into something underneath the collective unconscious, putting down our little wells into the aquifer.

Linda Connor

The computer needed something. In my house, no flat surface stays empty for long. Maggie Perry, my assistant, says these characters remind her of how creative computers can be. To me, they're like kiln gods, making sure our work survives the flames. I love their antiquated, idiosyncratic nature. The tall mud head came first, and that seemed to attract the others — its friends. It's a cottonwood carving for a clown kachina. Kachinas are models Hopis and Zunis originally made for their children, to show them what the gods looked like. Now they carve them mostly for tourists. I bought this one before it was painted; I liked it the way it was.

There's something about the dynamic of these small, spirited, pretechnological figures together that amuses me. They're quirky, they're odd little protectors, and Lord knows the computer needs protection. Maggie and I can use some protection from that computer, too.

CHAPTER  PLANTED OUTDOORS

I've hung some bells in the garden, small, quiet, metal ones from India and Nepal. Three are rusting; maybe they will disintegrate within a few years. I wonder what that will look like through the camera lens. I've photographed these bells over and over. First I had them hanging in the young oak trees. I didn't like the light tones of the bark; it contrasted too much with their dark metal green. I moved five bells to the pear tree, and photographed them at sunrise and sunset. Working with my slow film, it was hard to keep all the bells sharp; the small ones with fins attached to their clappers kept moving even in the slightest breeze. Lately I've hung a single bell on a pear tree branch just outside the bedroom window. We can see it when we are in bed, and I can photograph it from inside the room regardless of the weather. In my mind I observe the bell over years: in sunlight and moonlight, against winter branches and spring blossoms, on bright days and dull ones. I'm not sure now whether the bell or the pear tree is the shrine.

Sheila Neill

MY TREE

I'm an artist and a dancer—I spend a lot of time by myself. Having to build a new life as a single woman, a single mom, I turned to nature. I chose this tree because it's at the end of the road where I bike and walk. There were so few people here, I could have it all to myself. Also it's a perfect shape. The place where the branch was cut tilts back like an easel, and it has a cleft that can hold a branch or a stem. At first I used only things that grew wild in this area; now I include garden plants when I need the color. This morning I saw some beautiful tulips in a garden down the road. I knocked and the man who answered was so nice; he got his clippers and went right out and cut me this big yellow one.

People call this a shrine, but I don't. If you want to call it something, call it a paean, a song of praise. Or a poem to beauty. Or a poetic prayer. I would call it a prayer; I'm not afraid of that word. "Shrine" reminds me of certain religions. I was raised in the beautiful, romantic paganism of Catholicism. When I was twelve years old I asked a nun, "Isn't it a bit pagan to burn incense, light candles, wear special clothes, make gestures in the air, and speak in a language hardly anybody knows?" She said, "You're eccentric! I'm not talking to you!" and she went away. I feel slightly magical because of my Celtic background; I probably had a druid ancestry. Actually, I am a druid.

Sherry Kafka Wagner

TEXAS FENCE

The fence is fun because I get to say, "I'm going to straighten up Texas." The first time I said that I laughed and thought, Gosh, what a wonderful thing. Because anybody who knows me knows I can't resist; I'm always trying to straighten up Texas. "If you'd just listen to me, things would be a lot straighter around here."

That fence is an homage to time. I'm watching what falls off and how things change. I've had this stuff for years, and now it's time for it to go outside. I don't care if it all goes away. My sister was telling me that an old apple peeler out there is quite valuable. People are paying a lot of money for them. I said, "Well, if you want to take it down and take it to the antique store, it's fine with me." She said, "It's just going to rust out there." And I said, "I know that." Maybe it shouldn't be allowed to rust, but I had a space up there. I looked around for something that could go outside, and I decided on the apple peeler.

Things have already changed a lot since I put everything up two years ago. Colors, for example. The bird houses used to have little bands of color on them, and so did the little wooden figures. They had this wonderful purple color and now the paint's flaking off. The small clay pots are getting whiter. That big bamboo cathedral on the left—I've had that for almost thirty years. I wanted to put it out there; it's expendable. Come Christmas I'll go out and put candles in it. I'll put candles in all that stuff and light them all and it will look pretty for one night. All those things are out there in the world, taking their time.

Sylvia Luftig

SHRINE FOR BECKY

After our daughter, Becky, died in a car accident, Dennis and I and her brother, Josh, knew we were going to have a memorial for her, here in the heart of the garden. We had the willow arbor already; the leaves were just beginning to sprout. At the memorial, people added pictures and mementos, like beads and that pair of earrings on the white ceramic Madonna. Becky always traveled with those moccasins the Madonna is holding. I put Becky's picture with some pink paper flowers at the top, above a little shrine with the Virgin of Guadalupe that I'd made for her a few years back, when she graduated from college. I've always collected things and made shrines. I must have been a Catholic in some other life.

For the first six weeks after Becky died we'd come out here every night, light the candles and the tiki torches, and have a fire. We knew we wanted to stay here at home; that was important. This shrine is at the heart of our land, like your kids are the heart of your life. Becky believed in the Goddess; she was on a spiritual quest. I don't know what her path is now or where she is, but for me the shrine is a really strong connection to Becky. It's about comfort more than anything, comfort and beauty.

Anna Rucker

TOGETHER

To me making a shrine means showing people who you are, who you respect, who you like. Mainly, it can tell everything about you! I make shrines from different things that symbolize me; I'm an artist and a student in the seventh grade. Some of the shrines I make are happy, some aren't. The happy ones are just that I'm happy. I'm glad for what I have, my family, my friends, just life. If I was in a sad mood, I would probably make a sad kind of thing. We have a lot of devil and dead kind of stuff I could use.

This is a town, and the middle part symbolizes what goes on and what the different people do there. The branches on the stone cottage in the back are very special because the tree that they came from in our garden was cut down. The little people in the front symbolize . . . I guess it's just for decoration, the front thing. But then I put the necklace there because I really like that it shows the togetherness of the village. That all the houses and the people were connected.

Ken Botto

FIRE SALE GARDEN GODDESS

She's a Thai greeting figure. I wanted to put her in a good spot, so she's in the garden where I pass her every day. I found her in a yard sale on my own street; they had a huge collection of stuff. It had already been picked over, but leaning against the fence was this charred, carved, wooden figure that stood out among all the junk. Look at it! It's very sculptural. It's unique. And I like the way it's been burnt—it has a nice patina to it. Actually, that enhanced it. So when I look at the unburned ones in Thai restaurants now, they look kind of ordinary to me. They don't have the quality she has.

Wassana Boondtin Foreman

THAI SPIRIT HOUSE

I came here from Thailand in 1963. At least 99 percent of the people there have a spirit house. We believe that the soul doesn't die. In Thailand, when you pass by a temple or a spirit house, you put your hands up in prayer. My spirit house is for all the spirits of the dead. First, it's for the people who lived in this place before me. The land belonged to somebody else—I have to appreciate them. "I've come to your place; I have business here. Thanks; I'll keep the house clean, do nice things for the property."

You also have the spirit house especially for your mother and father. You pray for them when you have time, you think of something good to offer them. Flowers, candles, incense—we have to give them gifts. Sometimes I dream that the spirits in the spirit house want something. So I'll go and pick it up—food, merchandise, anything. When I talk to them, it makes me feel good inside. "I give this to you; please give what I want back to me." I also ask them to help me be good while I am alive. Never forget your ancestors from way back, or anybody who gave you even one bite of food!

I put the man at the door of the house to be a guardian, to protect us from any bad things around here. The man and woman inside are like souls that come there to find happiness. The turtle shell is from a turtle that came like magic, walking to my feet when I lived in Alameda. I said, "Oh my God, I have to pick him up and play with him!" He made me happy, so I keep his body in the spirit house. Animals have a soul when they die, too.

CHAPTER **5** PERSONAL ICONS

Today any image or representation may be called an icon. In computer terminology, for example, an icon is a picture on the screen that represents a particular command. Our personal icons are supposed to inspire us, reminding us, even commanding us, to try harder and be better, or perhaps to take it easier and be kinder to everyone, even ourselves. Some people venerate holy figures; others enshrine more human sources of inspiration.

In the week before the equinox and Easter this year, I began my shrine to spring with an icon—the Virgin of Guadalupe, who represents compassion. I found her imprinted on a calendar advertising the Tienda Guadalupe, a small shop in San Antonio, Texas. The Virgin is the patron saint of this shop, which sells "Art from the good folk of Texas, Mexico, and other sovereign nations." In front of her I placed an offering of Easter egg chocolates wrapped in bright foil, arranged in a black, footed bowl my friend Norma made for me thirty years ago.

Looking at the Virgin through the camera, I noticed that the cheap, shiny paper, rippled from being rolled and packed in my carry-on baggage, reflected the morning light like a mist gathering behind her. Four tiny ovals in the corners of the calendar show the Virgin's mythic history. First, she appears to Juan Diego, a peasant in sandals. Juan tries to run away. Then he kneels before her. In the last vignette, Juan, still in his sandals, is holding an image of the Virgin that seems to be imprinted on a cloak. He stands in a palace, before the archbishop. Roses, the traditional symbol of the Virgin, are strewn on the floor. Two priests hold up their hands in amazement; the archbishop has fallen to his knees.

Janet Carter

WORKING ALTAR FOR THE LUNAR NEW YEAR

The process of making a personal altar is thrilling. It's really a passion for me. I made my first altars when I was teaching astrology in the early 1980s. It was easier for students to understand certain concepts—say, the particular qualities of each planet, or of the four elements—when I could show them with objects. To evoke the feeling of fire as an element, I might arrange a red cloth, a sun mask, candles, chili peppers, and other hot, fiery things. To illustrate earth I could use rocks, stalks of wheat, pennies and other metallic objects, fruits, and vegetables. Creating these teaching aids inspired me to start working with altars in a more personal way.

The power of an altar, the way objects come to be on it, is mysterious and fascinating. I set this altar up to work with certain issues and invite certain things into my life. The Matisse painting of the sensual woman, the photograph of me as a baby, and the photograph of my female lineage, including my grandmother, who is very traditional and repressed, all represent aspects of me. The shell Sharon gave me and the rock from Robert represent the two people closest to me; the gemstones in the shell are the richness of my connection with the two of them. The snake and the lizard are my allies, my protectors. I place all these objects on the altar in a way that represents their relationship to each other in my life.

Making an altar is making a relationship with objects in the world and the forces they possess. As humans we tend to imbue things with power and meaning—but objects also have their own essence. Even when I'm not sitting in front of it, my altar is working because these particular objects are activated by my intent. It's up to me to remember that the altar is here, to sit with it and take it in, not only with my mind but with my heart and body. The altar brings these three together.

Marina Golitzin

MY MOTHER'S ICONS

My mother, the Princess Golitzin, brought these icons with her when we had to leave Russia. I was a small child, but I remember quite a bit; it's nice to remember things. In 1917 we left Moscow—mother, father, and the children; we were three sisters and two brothers. We brought three servants as well. All of us went by train, with my father's cousin's family and a few others. I'm sure the icons were in the suitcase my mother kept with her. We brought only a few things, mostly in trunks—clothing, some household utensils, tablecloths, and linen. We arrived in the little town of Tyumen, just over the Ural Mountains, in Siberia. Later we moved farther east, to Krasnoyarsk.

In the winter of 1919 we heard that the Red Army was coming closer, and we traveled east to China in a boxcar. We left just before Christmas, and we didn't arrive in Harbin until April—five months to travel those several thousand miles! There was a shortage of coal, and there weren't enough engines. We would wait for weeks in a village, or a beautiful thick forest, or a field, for an engine to come along and take us farther. For us, the children, it was an adventure. In the

boxcar there were bunk beds and a potbellied stove. Of course, mother didn't put the icons out; it was too dangerous. They were not precious materially—I don't think icons were very expensive in Russia then—but they were precious for her. Later, in Harbin, the icons were in her bedroom, and after we emigrated to the United States in 1923, they were in our house in Seattle.

In Russia they say you should put the icons in the right corner of the room where you enter the house. Almost every room in our house there had at least one small shrine in a corner. Mother's icons were always on a little corner table near her bed. Even in Siberia, we would come to her room and say our prayers in front of them at night. In the morning she usually had her tea or coffee in bed; we would come in, all the children, and kiss her good morning, and make the sign of the cross. The icons were right there, and in 1948, when she died, they were in mother's and father's room in Los Angeles.

When my husband and I moved to northern California, we put the icons here in the right corner of the dining room. My mother's parents gave her the large one as a blessing when she got married. Mother brought the embroidered cloth with her from Russia, too. It's very old, 1911. When we lived on our estate, she had a workshop for women from the village. She sent the things they made to a crafts shop in Moscow, where they would sell them and get a little money for the women. The candles are from our church, and the rosaries are my daughter Natasha's, from her high school.

I asked Natasha, "What do you want to do with the icons when I die? Shall I will them to someone?" She said, "No, no, I want to keep them." You see, she grew up in the house with these things, she remembers them. My mother used to take her to the Russian Orthodox Church all the time. I was not as religious as mother was. I don't go to church at all now because I'm ninety—just too darn old. In Russia we used to go every Sunday. We had a beautiful church on our estate, but it was very close to where Stalin lived. And he could see the cupola. He didn't like that, and in 1930 the church was destroyed. There are no ruins left, just grass.

José Araújo

In the countryside of Brazil, where I'm from, people have images of Catholic saints in their houses. It's a kind of cult of the saints that is Catholic and at the same time pagan. My mother is very Catholic, big on altars and shrines, and as a Catholic kid I was given a lot of medals, crosses, little statues of different saints. So I began collecting them early. When I went to the seminary, I would keep them in my room in a little bag or hidden away in my closet.

Later I learned about the Afro-Brazilian religions, especially Umbanda and Candomble. They are even more animistic than Catholicism. The Africans who came to Brazil as slaves were able to maintain their religions despite the repression. One way they did that was by using Catholic images to signify their deities. So Saint Sebastian is the Candomble Oxossi, the Virgin Mary is Yemenja, and Saint Anthony is Exu.

I see this *Altar-Mor* as a concentration of energy, like the altar in a temple, where you can replenish your powers and make offerings to the spirits that surround and protect you. Sete Flechas (Seven Arrows) is at the center. He's one of the best known of the *cablocos*, the spirits of the Brazilian Native Americans. He is a cowboy, a protector. I have beads here from various temples, pictures of my dead friends, some water from Lourdes, flowers from our wedding, rocks from the riverbed where I was born. And the Virgin of Fatima, who represents the Catholicism of my mother.

I have another shrine, the *Casa dos Exus*, a very simple one. These are its elements: incense for burning, offerings of rum, red candles, partly smoked cigars, and the *exus*, or messengers. They are the spirits who do the ordinary tasks for you. That shrine includes Ze Pilintra, the spirit of one of the characters in Rio they call "the bums." They're not really bums; they're streetwise people. The whole thing about Umbanda is that it acts as a kind of liberating venue for poor people. In Umbanda ceremonies the highest spirits usually manifest themselves as the ones considered the lowest in society—the prostitutes, the bums, the pirates, the outcasts. They become great, and they come as healers to help the people.

Michelle Valladares

UNTITLED PERSONAL ALTAR

I was raised as a Catholic in India and Kuwait. I grew up around different religions, and many of the homes I entered as a child had altars. I remember that my mother had a wooden Virgin Mary hanging over her bed, and my grandmother had a Virgin on a table with rosary beads, little Catholic artifacts, and a picture of my grandfather.

I built my first small shrine in New York five or six years ago. I had always constructed shrines unconsciously, on the top of my desk or dresser. When I married José, he knew a lot about Umbanda, a Brazilian religion that utilizes shrines and altars. We were both sort of secret shrine keepers, and one of the things we did for each other was to liberate our altars. José taught me a lot about physically setting up an altar, and he gave me some objects for my shrine, but I wouldn't consider it an Umbanda shrine. It's mostly just for me, or to help friends or family who are sick or in trouble. And for José when he is traveling. I put their pictures on the altar so that I can pray for them or give them my good energy. I keep the wedding picture of my grandparents nearby because I think it's important to honor and remember them.

When I'm working at my desk I always light the candles and the incense because I feel that my altar is a sort of doorway, the path to good intentions. I really believe these things help, so I give the altar a lot of care and attention. It is a way of feeding the spirits. Every now and then, I dust and clean everything, light all the candles, put out fresh water. Just as you would weed a garden. I do this when I feel I need help, and also when I receive help and want to say thanks. For me the altar is alive, full of vitality and spirit, and it needs to be cared for. The more you feed it, the more it will come alive for you.

Araceli Ferolino Williams

MY SANTO NIÑO SHRINE

I got this little Santo Niño figure as a gift from a friend. Over in the Philippines we believe that it's better to get a saint as a gift—if you buy one on your own, it has a different feeling. The original Santo Niño statue was a gift brought by Ferdinand Magellan when he came to the Philippines on March 16, 1521. He gave it to the Queen of Cebu, who ruled in the central part of the Philippines. When the queen accepted it, her gesture indicated that the foreigners were welcome to the island. But it was also a gesture of accepting the new religion because during those days we—the natives—had our own beliefs, in nature. That was the beginning of Christianity in the Philippines. And ever since then people worship or pray to the Santo Niño, which we still believe is a miraculous image.

Literally, Santo Niño is like the infant Jesus, a child who is always honest and always tries to help you, even though sometimes he may not be able to do it. Filipinos believe that their prayers to Santo Niño are heard; they ask for help and make wishes, like for good health and good fortune. I myself believe that the Santo Niño does help. To this day, we celebrate the Feast of the Santo Niño on the third Sunday of January.

That Bible was given to me by a neighbor of ours when I was twenty-nine, on the day we were notified that one of my brothers was killed. That was just one month after my father died. She told me, "This will help you. Keep this Bible wherever you go." And so I kept it; it's right here with me now. The little crucifix was given to us by Dwight, my husband Rudy's boss at the restaurant. The crucifix is always a symbol of Christianity, no matter what faith you belong to. We have two crucifixes that were blessed by the pope. The crucifix lying on the table I bought here in San Antonio. I could not take the one from our family altar in the Philippines; it's the only one we have there. I also have the different novenas here. I have a Mother of Perpetual Help—I pray to that every Wednesday. I have my St. Jude—I pray to that on Thursdays, and then on Fridays I have the Santo Niño. If I have time, I pray every day to the Holy Rosary. And sometimes when I get so tired I might fall asleep any minute, I just pray while lying down. I think Christ or God will understand.

Veronica Bhonsle

GOD HOUSE

Our family is very eclectic, so I guess this god house represents how open you can be to different philosophies. I was raised in Bolivia; my parents were Bolivian and my grandfather was Italian. We had the Inca—the Indian—influence, but I grew up with the Catholic religion. We always had saints, and Jesus and Pacha Mama (Mother Earth) to pray to in the house. After I left for the United States, my grandmother would send me a Virgin whenever things got tough. She would tell me I'd better pray; the Virgin would protect me.

I think it was after Sunil and I got married that I started doing my own shrine. It was just part of making a home, and then the shrine got bigger and bigger. Now we have a multicultural god house; that's what you see here. What I like about it is that they all get along in there—the Virgins, the Hindu figures, the Buddhas, the Native American things. My husband is Hindu. The last time we went to India, we went to a temple to have our marriage blessed. The man who performed the ceremony gave us a coconut as a sign of his blessing, for good luck. So we came home from India with our coconut.

Sherry Kafka Wagner

PLACE OF CONNECTIONS, OF AMUSEMENT AND INTEREST

I love that expression on my father's face. He's saying, "Oh Sherry, you've got a lot of interesting junk up here." That was his attitude toward life, really, always a little amused and interested. Not interested and amused, but first amused and *then* interested. When I moved here I would run across things as I was unpacking that I didn't really know what to do with. All of them had some sort of special meaning; they were given to me as a present or I had gotten them in a way that was significant. I started putting them all on the dresser just because it was a flat surface.

Everything I put here was personal, and I began to think of this as a kind of spiritual place, a spiritual expression. Everything on this chest is about me, or speaks to me, in some way; it's from my *internal* past. The other surfaces in my house are filled with enormous numbers of things from my *external* past. They're about the world and my appreciation and love of that world—my collection of edge objects, for example, where materials from the First World have been transformed by Third World people into something else. That's about objects and materials; it expresses ideas about culture.

I was never really *thinking*, I was just *doing*, when I put things in that lovely, flat basket. It was woven by the Tohono O'Odham; they're the great Indian basket weavers outside of Tucson. I do remember thinking that my granddaughter Tory and I would have a good time going through all these little stones and things I picked up on the beach. And we have. Every so often she says, "I want to look at all the things in the basket." She's not big enough to see it, so I have to lift her. We go through all the things, and then we put them back. My great-grandmother had a button box and as a child I spent countless hours playing with it, looking at the buttons, wondering where they came from, making designs, and just fiddling with them. I think that's why I like to have so many things as an adult.

Look at this Native American stone carving of an eagle. I had the most amazing dream of my life, a perfectly wonderful dream about writing and about my children, that centered around this eagle. He even had a name, *Kyrie Eleison*. I go back to that dream a lot. Some tribes believe that a vision of your totem, your significant animal, can come in a dream. I decided that it must have been my totem dream; the eagle is my totem. That's why I have the small, beaded Zuni eagle dancer. When you take the headdress off, there's his little human face.

I bought the figure of El Niño, the baby Jesus, because I love the story of how he wears out his shoes going around doing good works. It's such a realistic thing. If you go around doing good works, you wear out your shoes, you know what I mean? There is a price to be paid for good works, as for everything.

Once, when someone commented that I have so many necklaces, Cy, my former husband, said, "Oh no, no. Sherry doesn't have jewelry. She has stories." That's the way it is with all my objects. My impulse is not primarily aesthetic. It's not the look of the object, it's the story the object embodies for me. Of course the textures of the things in my jewelry box all mingle well. But I don't have that exquisite sensibility of placing things that some people have. I just drop things here. And if it holds, okay.

Of course things on the dresser change; they change all the time. But everything I put here connects in some way to me or to my relationship with other people, since so much of it has been given to me. It is about making connections in time, connections with place and connections with people. And there are connections with ideas, too. I see certain ideas when I look at everything up here. I've always been interested in every person's inherent creativity, our relationship to the world, our connection to everything else in creation.

Va'sih Tim hich, Violet Ruth Super

MY ELVIS HOUSE

Va'sihTini hich is my Karuk name; I'm a full-blooded Karuk, an elder of the Karuk tribe of California. An old Karuk lady willed me this name before she died. I say it means "wide back," and I don't like to be called that. My niece Jeanerette says it means "strong back, good for carrying wood." I've always worked hard, until the last few years—I'll be eighty on my next birthday.

I started losing my eyesight in 1949, when I was in my thirties, but I was able to see Elvis clearly enough. The first time I saw a picture of him was in 1954, when my husband Leonard's nephew Kenny Super came home from the service on furlough. He brought us a record—"Heartbreak Hotel." After that Leonard bought other Elvis records, and we saw all of his movies more than twice. I've been to Graceland, too; we stayed at the Elvis Motel there. This house is filled with Elvis. I have caps and jackets and spoons and socks and bath towels, two or three clocks, two Elvis dolls, lots and lots of pictures. I have little guitars that sing when you turn them on. I do that once in a while and it sounds just like Elvis. One guitar plays "Blue Christmas." It really is a blue Christmas without him.

I miss him. There was something good and clean about Elvis—the way he sang and the way he moved around. He had nice, beautiful songs and his movies were all clean, no fighting, just a lot of singing. But even with all the success around him, in his heart he seemed sad. If you listen to the songs, he was singing to his ex-wife. At the end he got real heavy, and he didn't sing anymore. All the pictures I have are when he was young. It's so sad—I think of him all the time.

Ken Botto

KITCHEN SINK SHRINE

Well, first of all, these aren't women. They're images; they stand for something else. They tell something about us and how we see. At the center, right below the Venus de Milo, are a little bride and groom. They are actually porcelain, Japanese-made. The shop must have had at least a dozen of them, all lined up with other things in the window. They were expensive, something like twenty-five dollars. Of course, you can also get cheapo spin-offs, but the Japanese ones have the detail. I didn't want to spend that much, but I noticed that one was broken. One of the grooms didn't have a head! That was more interesting than the regular ones. I got it cheap, maybe five bucks or something. And then as I left, I don't know why, I noticed that the little head had fallen down on one of the lower shelves. So I went back and got my head! I decided, why put it back on his shoulders? I'll just put the head in the bride's arm.

It's probably about marriage. When you're dealing with these figures, it takes you into relationships. What can I learn about myself by putting these things together? How did they come into being, what does that pose represent? You know, I have all these gay and lesbian figures on my refrigerator and after a while it seems like they're all part of the same pot. They're all parts of ourselves, like a mirror. All this stuff is a mirror.

Lora Amara

CORPORATE LADDER HONORING THE GODDESS

This ladder honors women and the transformation they can bring to the world. It's amusing to call it a "corporate ladder" because, as you can see, it's just an old paint-splattered ladder. I was attracted to the quirkiness of it. I liked that it was a well-used ladder, and the shape and the red color appealed to my designer eye. The cards depict the stories of women who have opened up space for our lives to be as full and free as we like. I began by hanging the cards from strings, but then I realized that they really needed a single thread running through all of them. So I used an unbroken piece of wire.

I keep the ladder between my bed and my chair, where I have to walk past it every day, and every day I think about the women. Whenever you do anything like this, as anybody who builds altars knows, the things speak to you after you place them. The women on these cards really stood up for themselves; you can see it in their faces and how they carry themselves. All I have to do is look at these women, and I realize that I'm not alone, I'm one of a long lineage.

CHAPTER  6 MEDITATING

I built this bench of Douglas fir. A beginner's simple design. In the morning I sit in front of it on my round black zafu for half an hour, unless I am desperately late, when I leave with a brief, apologetic bow to the little old Buddha from Thailand. Most of the time I think of her as a woman. Above her head are wooden beads from Nina that spell "S E E." My friend Elaine left the basket of ghosts on our doorstep one Halloween years ago when she was in her ghost pe-riod, making hundreds of little ghosts with ink-dot eyes from pieces of sheet she tied with red thread. The cracked stone, which reminds me of an Irish megalith, was a gift from Linda. The dark, dried-up things at its foot are flowers from my son Mark's wedding two years ago—an orchid from my corsage and the rose Doug wore in his lapel. Beth, my daughter, pinched a little ball of clay to make the blue incense pot when she was in first grade. She is thirty-three now.

Polly Schaafsma

ESSENTIAL FOCUS SHRINE

This is a collection of objects with spiritual relevance. I think of it as a shrine because it focuses on landscapes and places that are particularly significant for me. That's why I have the fossils and the potsherd from the Colorado Plateau, for example. The plateau and the Pueblo world are ongoing sources of inspiration, as are the Himalayas. The horsehair with the cloth sewn into it is something I happened to find in Ladakh, India, on a trail in the Zanskar Range. People there sew prayers in cloth into their horses' manes—to bring the horses good luck, I assume. I see this as expressing continuity and connection between themselves and their animals, and by extension all other life. I like that.

Hidden inside those baskets are animal fetishes and some other private things. Being hidden adds to the power of objects and places. Hidden things have an ambiguity and uncertainty about them—knowing that something is hidden suggests the presence of something deeper and greater than what you can see. I began to realize that during a Pueblo village excavation, when we found artifacts that had been deposited in the course of building the houses. Objects—spiritual treasures—were left as prayers and blessings inside these structures. When you go into a pueblo, or maybe into any tribal habitation or ancient village, it's not just what meets the eye, it's the sense that things are embedded—the turquoise in the wall or under the floor, the handprint purposely left in the adobe—that makes that place sacred and powerful. You feel something going on that is not happening in American houses built by contractors!

To me, this shrine is a grounding place in a world that is utterly crazy. Nothing on it ties into any formal, organized religion—not even Buddhism. It is more of a free-spirit sort of thing, not confined by dogma. Landscape and place are more important than dogma—these objects remind me of that.

Robert (Bow-Lun) Lew

MAHAYANA BUDDHA SHRINE

That's a very, very old little Buddha, about three hundred years old, given to me by my grandmother before she died. She brought it from China when our family emigrated during the Cultural Revolution; I was ten years old. This Buddha is on a small scale because I want to stay within the scale of my house. Actually, in some homes the Buddha is a huge presence; it isn't a little dinky Buddha like this one. But this is a cottage, not a big mansion. So why put a big Buddha in a little teeny house?

Those special porcelain cups hold the three essences: air, fire, and water. They add to the sacrament of purifying the altar. The original structure was a project I did for an advanced structures class at the university. I brought it home and I thought, hmm, I'd better utilize it in some way instead of just having it sit in one corner doing nothing. So it lent itself to turning into a little shrine.

I started by burning incense, just to purify the space. Then I set the Buddha on a board. When you create a shrine, you need objects and supporting articles to elevate the Buddha. You don't just put the image on a flat surface. So I found a piece of marble and a little board for the dais and then I added another little marble piece, right underneath the Buddha. You can just have these things around the house; you don't have to go and buy them.

Of course you always have to create a backdrop for the Buddha. I wanted the backdrop to reflect light. I had this gold foil tray, which is perfect, because many Asian shrines are actually gilded. You also need a piece of fabric to soften the hard edge of the gold. I used red because it's the base chakra, which is the beginning of life, in one sense. It's also a happy color. It stands for longevity, or fertility, and good fortune, all of those. Red and gold are often used together. Behind the backdrop I store some of the things that you use when you're actually meditating. One is a bell you strike three times very softly when you're opening the meditation. That's to quiet your soul, bring your psyche and your spirit into the realm of the Buddha.

Victoria Scott

MEDITATION SHRINE

This is the shrine my husband, Tony Misch, made for me, where I sit each morning. He once called it the "cockpit to enlightenment." He knew that I liked little Buddhas; that's why he made those small niches. He used the saffron and maroon because they are the Tibetan Buddhist colors, and he made the little shelves so I could put some papers underneath. The shrine is situated so that when I sit on the cushion I can also just see over the windowsill out onto the mountains.

The number of pieces in it has grown over the years. And every time I dust, which is maybe once a year, things shift around a bit. That little vase I put the matches in—that's probably my oldest possession, which I remember from when I was two or three years old. And the small tiger was made by my mother-in-law, who was very dear to me. So it represents Tony's mother as well as being charming in itself. The image in the center with the heart and columns is a valentine Tony made for me. Some of the things are made by Nina and Cia, our daughters. Most of the Buddhas are thrift shop Buddhas, or were given to me, or I found them here and there. The larger one on the windowsill, for example, was in a shop window in Siena with women's underwear draped over it. I'd just bought some nice little plastic St. Catherines of Siena from a souvenir stand outside the Duomo and that Buddha seemed to want to come along, too.

Even if it's only some little plastic thing in a souvenir stand, when there are multiple figures I always look at every single one. I choose the one where the pupils of the eyes are painted on in a way that looks at you, that isn't cockeyed or vacuous. If there's one that conveys warmth, that's the one I take. If the mold has been used too many times, or the colors are too garish, or if it's been stepped on, it won't have the charming quality of kitsch, much less the ability to say, "I am representing compassion." It may do in a pinch, but if I have my choice, I always choose the one that still has the aesthetic and, I guess, iconographic *oomph.*

Zann Goff

GRAPE CRATE ALTAR

I made this altar from a grape crate I got at Whole Foods, where I work. I was really fascinated by the triptychs at a Greek orthodox store down on Mission Street, but I couldn't afford those. So I came up with my own; I just hinged two planks onto the crate. My original plan was to carve the planks into gothic points, but I'm not that handy with a saw. I left them shaped as they are, and painted them with colors left over from painting the bedroom. Then I attached the Renaissance postcards and painted on the gold halos.

Especially on full moons and solstices and equinoxes, I'll just pull up a chair and light the candle and incense and sit here. Every couple of weeks, I change that little sculpturing model at the top. It goes with my moods. If I'm up, it has a free-flowing form. If I'm feeling more depressed, it tends to look very stoic, either rigid or bent in some uncomfortable pose. I etched the mirror with the bird in high school. The pope was given to me by my friend Beth. It's a fan she got at Mission Dolores for fifty cents. More of a kitsch factor than anything else, but it seemed a natural thing to have in a somewhat religious altar. There's also a bottle of holy water and some crucifixes.

Adam and I seem to be creating shrines all over the house now. It hasn't been entirely intentional, but we notice after we set up a little area with knickknacks and so on that it looks altaristic. Everybody should have an altar, or a specific place where they can go to meditate. I think everybody does, whether they realize it or not. Maybe it's just their knickknack shelf or curio cabinet, but most people have a place where they conglomerate things that are special to them. A place that centers them, whether they're conscious of meditating in front of it or just sitting there watching TV and spacing out.

Acknowledgments

THANKS TO:

Douglas Muir, husband and partner, essential to my work and life.

My children: Beth Stein, witty, incisive reviewer; Mark Stein, ideal photographic collaborator;

his wife, Karen O'Donnell Stein, superb copy editor; and Heather Muir, astute adviser.

All the talented shrine makers, including the ones whose work, finally, did not fit into this book.

Carol Field, who inspired, informed, and encouraged me again and again.

Barbara Ras, whose advice was instrumental early on.

Ina Evans, whose brilliant critiques I have long depended upon.

Norma Ashby, Bronni Galin, Christine Guthrie, Elaine James, Tobey Robertson, and Naomi Weissman,

close friends who have helped me and cheered me on for twenty years or longer.

Whitney Chadwick, Linda Connor, and Eleanor Coppola for their keen vision and useful comments.

Mary Felstiner, Diana Ketcham, Cyra McFadden, Annegret Ogden, Diana O'Hehir, and Alison Owings for

their generous criticism, praise, and copyediting.

Sherry Wagner, who housed, fed, and heartened me in Texas.

Victor Landweber, for his computer wizardry.

Judith Dunham, Lewis Watts, Richard Gordon, and Debra Heimerdinger for contributing their expertise.

Bonnie Nadell, my savvy agent, and Barbara and Oakley Hall, the good friends who helped me find her.

Bitsy Wright, my guide and sidekick in San Antonio.

Alfred Rucker for his remarkable artwork and our conversations about this project.

Diane and Jack Fulton, for her sharp proofreading, his salutary irreverence, and the loan of their red truck.

Meridel Rubenstein, Jerry West, Holly Roberts, and Bob Wilson for their art and hospitality.

I'Lee Hooker and my Thursday morning writing class for their friendship and enthusiasm.

Amy Smith for her impeccable transcriptions.

Julie Landweber for her perceptive editorial assistance.

Stephani Martinez for her Polaroid detective work.

Linda Stalter at Sieg Photographics and Karen and John Leung at CoLab for their professional skills.

My editors at Chronicle Books, Annie Barrows, Karen Silver, and especially Leslie Jonath,

who deftly brought the book into being.